CITIZENSHIP TEST PREP

100 CIVICS QUESTIONS
QUICK CIVICS LESSONS
READING VOCABULARY
WRITING VOCABULARY
CITIZENSHIP INTERVIEW
BRIEF AMERICAN HISTORY
HELPFUL RESOURCES

EVERYTHING YOU NEED TO KNOW!

Angelo Tropea

ISBN: 9798301050909

This book is a companion to our Study App

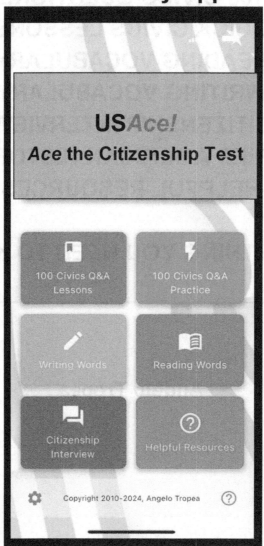

Welcome to
Citizenship Test Prep
Complete Preparation

Suggestions on how to use this book

First, get a "bird's eye view" of this book. Leaf through the pages so that you will become familiar with both the format and content of the book.

The first two sections deal with the Official Civics Questions and answers as published by the USCIS (Immigration and Naturalization Service)

The next section prepares you for the "Writing" part of the test. It has all the words that you need to know how to write.

The "Reading" section prepares you with all the words that you will need to know how to read.

The "Citizenship Interview" explains the interview process that you will need to undergo. It eliminates the "mystery" of the interview and includes helpful hints to help you ace the interview.

A "History of the U.S." will help you to associate the civics questions to the history of the U.S., making it easier for you to understand and memorize them.

The "Representatives and Capitals" sections provides you with a list of political representatives and state capitals. To answer some questions, you will need this information.

Helpful Resources" are links to sites that are useful in the citizenship preparation process.

Our most important tip:

Study every day until you feel ready for the Citizenship Test!

Good Luck!

100 Civics Q&A Lessons	100 Official Civics Questions and Answers in Question / Answer format for easy memorizing

One part of the U.S. naturalization test is the civics test. The applicant is asked up to ten civics questions from the one hundred questions published by the U.S. Citizenship and Immigration Services (USCIS).

The topics covered by these questions are American government, history, and civics, principles and structure of the United States. This includes questions on the U.S. Constitution, the branches of the American government, major historical events, the rights and responsibilities of citizens, and U.S. geography.

Applicants must answer at least six of the questions correctly to prove that they have a good understanding of America's history and democratic values.

To answer the questions correctly, applicants need to study the questions and answers. Some questions are easy, such as "What is the supreme law of the land?" or "Who was the first President of the United States?"

Other questions are harder, such as "What did the Emancipation Proclamation do?" or "What are two rights of everyone living in the United States?"

In this book we will cover all 100 questions and answers in various ways to help you understand and remember them.

Questions and Answers and Quick Civics Lessons

Question and Answer	Civics Lesson
1. What is the supreme law of the land? • *the Constitution*	The Constitution is the supreme (highest) law of the U. S. It was written in 1787 by the leaders of our government. It lists the rights of people who live in the U. S. It says that all laws in the U. S. must follow the Constitution.
2. What does the Constitution do? • *sets up the government* • *defines the government* • *protects basic rights of Americans*	The Constitution divides government power into two parts: national government and state governments. It also limits the power of each part by dividing the powers into three parts called "branches" (executive, legislative and judicial). The Constitution is made up of the original Constitution plus changes and additions called "amendments." The first 10 amendments, called the "Bill of Rights," established the rights and liberties of all Americans.

3. The idea of self-government is in the first three words of the Constitution. What are these words? • *We the People*	The first three words of the Constitution, "We the people," make clear that the people set up the government. The power of government comes from the people who are the highest power. People elect representatives to make laws. The government works for the people and protects the rights of people.

4. What is an amendment?
   • *a change (to the Constitution)*
   • *an addition (to the Constitution)*
	An amendment is a change or addition to the Constitution. The Constitution explains how an amendment can be made and added to the Constitution.

5. What do we call the first ten amendments to the Constitution? • *the Bill of Rights*	The Bill of Rights is the first 10 amendments to the Constitution. The amendments protect individual rights and place limits on the power of government.

6. What is one right or freedom from the First Amendment?*
   • *Speech*
   • *religion*
   • *assembly*
   • *press*
   • *petition the government*
	The First Amendment of the Constitution guarantees and protects freedom of speech and other rights.

7. How many amendments does the Constitution have? ● *twenty-seven (27)*	There are 27 amendments to the Constitution. These amendments include the first 10 amendments which are known as the "Bill of Rights."

8. What did the Declaration of Independence do?
    ● *announced our independence (from Great Britain)*
    ● *declared our independence (from Great Britain)*
    ● *said that the United States is free (from Great Britain)*
	The Declaration of Independence was written by Thomas Jefferson and accepted by the Second Continental Congress on July 4, 1776.
	It announced our independence from Great Britain (England) and also contains important ideas about the American system of government.

9. What are two rights in the Declaration of Independence?
    ● *Life*
    ● *liberty*
    ● *pursuit of happiness*
	The Declaration of Independence lists three rights that the Founding Fathers considered to be natural and "unalienable" (rights that cannot be taken away).
	They are the right to life, liberty, and the pursuit of happiness.

10. What is freedom of religion? • *You can practice any religion, or not practice a religion.*	One reason why colonists came to America was religious freedom. The First Amendment prohibits Congress from setting up an official U.S. religion and protects the rights of citizens to hold any religious belief, or none at all.
11. What is the economic system in the United States?* • *capitalist economy* • *market economy*	In the American economy, most businesses are privately owned. Competition, supply, and demand influence the decisions of businesses and consumers.
12. What is the "rule of law"? • *Everyone must follow the law.* • *Leaders must obey the law.* • *Government must obey the law.* • *No one is above the law.*	The rule of law means that everyone (citizens and leaders) must obey the laws. The rule of law helps to make sure that government protects all people equally and does not violate the rights of people.

13. Name one branch or part of the government.* • *Congress (legislative)* • *President (executive)* • *the courts (judicial)*	The three branches of government are: legislative, executive, and judicial. The legislative branch (Congress) makes laws. The executive branch (President) enforces the laws that Congress passes. The judicial branch decides if government laws and actions follow the Constitution.
14. What stops one branch of government from becoming too powerful? • *checks and balances* • *separation of powers*	The separation of government into three branches creates a system of checks and balances. This separation of powers limits the power of the government and prevents the government from violating the rights of the people
15. Who is in charge of the executive branch? • *the President*	The head of the executive branch is the president. The president signs treaties, selects ambassadors, sets national policies and proposes laws to Congress. The president names the top leaders of the federal departments and nominates a person when there is a vacancy on the Supreme Court.

16. Who makes federal laws? • *Congress* • *Senate and House (of representatives)* • *(U.S. or national) Legislature*	Either side of Congress - the Senate or the House of Representatives - can propose a bill to address an issue. If both houses approve the bill, it goes to the president to be signed into law. If the president signs the bill, it becomes a federal law.
17. What are the two parts of the U.S. Congress?* • *Senate and House (of Representatives)*	Congress is divided into two parts - the Senate and the House of Representatives. The system of checks and balances works in Congress and limits the power of each part.
18. How many U.S. Senators are there? • one hundred (100)	There are 100 senators in Congress, two from each state.
19. We elect a U.S. Senator for how many years? • *six (6)*	Senators serve for six years. Because of this, they are more independent of public opinion than Representatives who serve for two years.

20. Who is one of your state's U.S. Senators now?* • *Answers depends upon which state you live in*	*(District of Columbia residents and residents of U.S. territories should answer that D.C. (or the territory where the applicant lives) has no U.S. Senators.) (Visit senate.gov to find your state's U.S. Senators.)*
21. The House of Representatives has how many voting members? • *four hundred thirty-five (435)*	Each state must have at least one representative in the House. Beyond that, the number of representatives from each state depends on the population of the state. (Total Representatives: 435)
22. We elect a U.S. Representative for how many years? • *two (2)*	U.S. Representatives serve for short 2-year terms before they have to run for reelection. This encourages them to constantly stay in touch and reflect the views of the people that voted them in.
23. Name your U.S. Representative. • *Answers depend on where you live.*	*(Residents of territories with Non-voting delegates or resident commissioners may provide the name of that Delegate or Commissioner. Also acceptable is any statement that the territory has no (voting) Representatives in Congress.) (Visit house.gov to find your U.S. Representative.)*

24. Who does a U.S. Senator represent? • *all people of the state*	There are 2 U.S. Senators for each state. They are elected by all the voters in their state.
25. Why do some states have more Representatives than other states? • *(because of) the state's population* • *(because) they have more people* • *(because) some states have more people*	A state's population determines the number of representatives it has.
26. We elect a President for how many years? • *four (4)*	Early American leaders decided that the people would elect the president every four years. The president is the only official elected by the entire country through the Electoral College. The president can only be elected to two terms (four years each) for a total of eight years.
27. In what month do we vote for President?* • *November*	Election Day is the Tuesday after the first Monday in November.

28. What is the name of the President of the United States now?* • *Visit uscis.gov/citizenship/testupdates for the name of the President of the United States.*	For more information about the president of the United States, visit whitehouse.gov.
29. What is the name of the Vice President of the United States now? • *Visit uscis.gov/citizenship/testupdates for the name of the Vice President of the United States.*	For more information about the vice president of the United States, visit whitehouse.gov
30. If the President can no longer serve, who becomes President? • *the Vice President*	If the president dies, resigns, or cannot work while still in office, the vice president becomes president.
31. If both the President and the Vice President can no longer serve, who becomes President? • *the Speaker of the House*	If both the president and vice president cannot serve, the next person in line is the Speaker of the House of Representatives. The 25th Amendment established procedures for presidential and vice presidential succession.

32. Who is the Commander in Chief of the military? • *the President*	The president commands the armed forces, but Congress has the power to pay for the armed forces and declare war. Because of our system of three branches of government and our system of checks and balances, one branch of government is able to check the power of the other branches.
33. Who signs bills to become laws? • *the President*	If the president wants the bill to become law, he signs it. If the president does not want the bill to become law, he vetoes it.
34. Who vetoes bills? • *the President*	The president can reject a bill passed by Congress. If the president vetoes a bill, he prevents it from becoming a law. However, if two-thirds of the House and two-thirds of the Senate vote to pass the bill again, the bill becomes a law.

35. What does the President's Cabinet do? • *advises the President*	The Constitution says that the leaders of the executive departments should advise the president. These department leaders, most of them called "secretaries," make up the cabinet.
36. What are two Cabinet-level positions? • *Secretary of Agriculture* • *Secretary of Transportation* • *Secretary of Commerce* • *Secretary of Veterans Affairs* • *Secretary of Defense* • *Secretary of the Treasury* • *Secretary of Education* • *Secretary of the Interior* • *Secretary of Energy* • *Secretary of Labor* • *Secretary of Health and Human Services* • *Secretary of State* • *Secretary of Homeland Security* • *Attorney General* • *Secretary of Housing and Urban Development* • *Vice President*	The people on the president's cabinet are the vice president and the heads of the 15 executive departments.

37. What does the judicial branch do? • *reviews laws* • *explains laws* • *resolves disputes (disagreements)* • *decides if a law goes against the Constitution*	The judicial branch is one of the three branches of government. The Constitution established the judicial branch of government with the creation of the Supreme Court. Congress created the other federal courts. The courts review and explain the laws, and they resolve disagreements about the meaning of the law. The Supreme Court also rules on other cases, such as disagreements between states.
38. What is the highest court in the United States? • *the Supreme Court*	The U.S. Supreme Court has complete authority over all federal courts. The Supreme Court's interpretations of federal laws and of the Constitution are final. However, it cannot make decisions about state law or state constitutions unless a state law or action conflicts with federal law or with the U.S. Constitution. The Supreme Court also rules on cases about significant social and public policy issues that affect all Americans.

39. How many justices are on the Supreme Court? • *nine (9)*	The Constitution gives the president the power to nominate justices to the Supreme Court. The nominee must then be confirmed by the Senate. Justices serve on the court for life or until they retire. For more information on the Supreme Court, go to www.supremecourt.gov.
40. Who is the Chief Justice of the United States now? • *Visit uscis.gov/citizenship/testupdates for the name of the Chief Justice of the United States*	John G. Roberts, Jr. is the 17th chief justice of the United States. Judge Roberts became chief justice when he was 50.
41. Under our Constitution, some powers belong to the federal government. **What is one power of the federal government?** • *to print money* • *to declare war* • *to create an army* • *to make treaties*	The powers of government are divided between the federal government and the state governments. The Constitution gives the federal government the power to print money, declare war, create an army, and make treaties. Most other powers that are not given to the federal government in the Constitution belong to the states.

42. Under our Constitution, some powers belong to the states. What is one power of the states?
   • *provide schooling and education*
   • *provide protection (police, provide safety, fire departments)*
   • *give a driver's license*
   • *approve zoning and land use*
	Although each state has its own constitution, state constitutions cannot conflict with the U.S. Constitution.
	State governments hold powers not given to the federal government in the U.S. Constitution. Some powers of the state government are the power to create traffic regulations and issue driver's licenses.
	The Constitution also provides a list of powers that states do not have, such as states cannot coin (create) money. State and federal governments also share some powers, such as ability to tax people.

43. Who is the Governor of your state now? • *Answers will vary. (District of Columbia residents should answer that D.C. does not have a Governor.) Visit usa.gov/states-and-territories to find the Governor of your state.*	The governor's job in a state government is similar to the president's job in the federal government. The governor's duties and powers vary from state to state. The number of years a governor is elected to serve (called a "term") is four years. Exceptions are New Hampshire and Vermont, where governors serve for two years.

44. What is the capital of your state?* • *Answers vary. (District of Columbia residents should answer that D.C. is not a state and does not have a capital. Residents of U.S. territories should name the capital of the territory.)*	Each state or territory has its own capital. The state capital is where the state government conducts its business. Usually, the governor lives in the state's capital city.
45. What are the two major political parties in the United States?* • *Democratic and Republican*	The two major political parties are the Democratic Party and the Republican Party. During U.S. history, there have been other parties. Political party membership in the United States is voluntary. Parties are made up of people who organize to promote candidates for election and promote their views about public policies.
46. What is the political party of the President now? • *Visit uscis.gov/citizenship/testupdates for the political party of the President.*	Visit uscis.gov/citizenship/testupdates for the political party of the President and the name of the President..

47. What is the name of the Speaker of the House of Representatives now? • *Visit uscis.gov/citizenship/testupdates for the name of the Speaker of the House of Representatives.*	The speaker is second in line to the succession of the presidency after the vice president.
48. There are four amendments to the Constitution about who can vote. Describe one of them. • *Citizens eighteen (18) and older (can vote).* • *You don't have to pay (a poll tax) to vote.* • *Any citizen can vote. (Women and men can vote.)* • *A male citizen of any race (can vote).*	There are four amendments to the Constitution about voting. 1) The 15th Amendment permits American men of all races to vote. 2) The 19th Amendment gave women the right to vote. 3) The 24th Amendment made poll taxes (taxes to be allowed to vote) illegal. 4) The 26th Amendment lowered the voting age from 21 to 18.
49. What is one responsibility that is only for United States citizens?* • *serve on a jury* • *vote in a federal election*	Two responsibilities of U.S. citizens are to serve on a jury and vote in federal elections. Participation of citizens on a jury helps ensure a fair trial. Another important responsibility of citizens is voting. By voting, citizens are participating in the democratic process

50. Name one right only for United States citizens.
    • *vote in a federal election*
    • *run for federal office*
	U.S. citizens have the right to vote in federal elections and also run for a federal office. Only U.S. citizens can vote in federal elections.

51. What are two rights of everyone living in the United States?
    • *freedom of expression*
    • *freedom to petition the government*
    • *freedom of speech*
    • *freedom of worship*
    • *freedom of assembly*
    • *the right to bear arms*
	The Constitution and Bill of Rights give rights to all people living in the United States. The rights include freedom of expression, religion, speech, freedom of assembly (freedom to meet together), freedom to petition the government (ask the government for something), freedom of worship, right to bear arms
	  .

52. What do we show loyalty to when we say the Pledge of Allegiance?
    • *the United States*
    • *the flag*
	The flag is an important symbol of the United States. When we recite the Pledge of Allegiance to the flag, we usually stand facing the flag with the right hand over the heart.

53. What is one promise you make when you become a United States citizen? • *give up loyalty to other countries* • *defend the Constitution and laws of the United States* • *obey the laws of the United States* • *serve in the U.S. military (if needed)* • *serve (do important work for) the nation (if needed)* • *be loyal to the United States*	The Constitution gave Congress the power to establish naturalization rules. Congress made rules about how immigrants could become citizens. After an immigrant fulfills all of the requirements to become a U.S. citizen, the final step is to take an Oath of Allegiance at a naturalization ceremony, which includes the promises made in the answer to this question.
54. How old do citizens have to be to vote for President?* • *eighteen (18) and older*	In 1971, the 26th Amendment changed the minimum voting age from 21 to 18 for all federal, state, and local elections.
55. What are two ways that Americans can participate in their democracy? • *vote* • *run for office* • *join a political party* • *help with a campaign* • *join a civic group* • *join a community group* • *give an elected official your opinion on an issue* • *call Senators and Representatives* • *publicly support or oppose an issue or policy* • *write to a newspaper*	Citizens play an active part in their communities. When Americans engage in the political process, democracy stays alive and strong. There are many ways for people to be involved.

56. When is the last day you can send in federal income tax forms?* • *April 15*	The last day to send in your federal income tax to the Internal Revenue Service is April 15 of each year. The government uses these taxes to keep our country safe and secure. It also provides many benefits.
57. When must all men register for the Selective Service? • *at age eighteen (18)* • *between eighteen (18) and twenty-six (26)*	Today there is no draft, but all men between 18 and 26 must register with the Selective Service System. When a man registers, he tells the government that he is available to serve in the U.S. Armed Forces.
58. What is one reason colonists came to America? • *freedom* • *political liberty* • *religious freedom* • *economic opportunity* • *practice their religion* • *escape persecution*	In the 1600s and 1700s, colonists from England and other European countries sailed across the Atlantic Ocean to the American colonies. The American colonies were a chance for freedom and a new life. Today, many people come to the U.S. for these reasons.
59. Who lived in America before the Europeans arrived? • *American Indians* • *Native Americans*	American Indian tribes such as the Navajo, Sioux, Cherokee, and Iroquois lived in America when the Pilgrims arrived. After much violence, the settlers defeated the Indian tribes and took much of their land.

60. What group of people was taken to America and sold as slaves?
   • *Africans*
   • *people from Africa*
	By 1700, many Africans were being brought to the American colonies as slaves. Slavery created a challenge for a nation founded on individual freedoms and democratic beliefs.
	It was one of the major causes of the American Civil War

61. Why did the colonists fight the British?
   • *because of high taxes (taxation without representation)*
   • *because the British army stayed in their houses (boarding, quartering)*
   • *because they didn't have self-government*
	Great Britain's "repeated injuries" against the Americans, as noted in the Declaration of Independence, convinced many to join the rebellion. The colonists believed the British did not respect their basic rights.
	The British governed the colonists without their consent, denying them self-government.

62. Who wrote the Declaration of Independence? • *(Thomas) Jefferson*	Thomas Jefferson wrote the Declaration of Independence in 1776. He was a very important political leader and thinker and third president of the United States.

63. When was the Declaration of Independence adopted? • *July 4, 1776*	To "adopt" the declaration of Independence means to accept the declaration as binding. In 1774, representatives from 12 of the 13 colonies met in Philadelphia, Pennsylvania and wrote the Declaration of Independence, On July 4, 1776, the Second Continental Congress adopted the Declaration of Independence.
64. There were 13 original states. Name three. • *New Hampshire* • *Delaware* • *Massachusetts* • *Maryland* • *Rhode Island* • *Virginia* • *Connecticut* • *North Carolina* • *New York* • *South Carolina* • *New Jersey* • *Georgia* • *Pennsylvania*	The 13 original states were all former British colonies. Today, the United States has 50 states

65. What happened at the Constitutional Convention? • *The Constitution was written.* • *The Founding Fathers wrote the Constitution.*	From May to September 1787, fifty-five delegates from 12 of the original 13 states (except for Rhode Island) met and created the Constitution which set up the new American government.
66. When was the Constitution written? • *1787*	The Constitution, written in 1787, created a new system of U.S. government - the same system we have today. By 1790, all 13 states had ratified the Constitution.
67. The Federalist Papers supported the passage of the U.S. Constitution. Name one of the writers. • *(James) Madison* • *(Alexander) Hamilton* • *(John) Jay* • *Publius*	The Federalist Papers were 85 essays that were printed in New York newspapers while New York State was deciding whether or not to support the U.S. Constitution. The essays were written in 1787 and 1788.

68. What is one thing Benjamin Franklin is famous for? • *U.S. diplomat* • *oldest member of the Constitutional Convention* • *first Postmaster General of the United States* • *writer of "Poor Richard's Almanac"* • *started the first free libraries*	Benjamin Franklin was one of the most influential Founding Fathers of the United States. He was the oldest delegate to the Constitutional Convention and one of the signers of the U.S. Constitution.
69. Who is the "Father of Our Country"? • *(George) Washington*	George Washington is called the Father of Our Country. He was the first American president. He presided over the Constitutional Convention in Philadelphia in 1787.
70. Who was the first President?* • *(George) Washington*	George Washington was the first president of the United States. He served for two terms, beginning in 1789.
71. What territory did the United States buy from France in 1803? • *the Louisiana Territory* • *Louisiana*	In 1803, the United States bought the Louisiana Territory from France for $15 million. The Louisiana Purchase doubled the size of the United States and expanded it westward.

72. Name one war fought by the United States in the 1800s.
    • *War of 1812*
    • *Mexican-American War*
    • *Civil War*
    • *Spanish-American War*
	The United States fought four major wars in the 1800s (the War of 1812, the Mexican-American War, the Civil War, and the Spanish-American War.

73. Name the U.S. war between the North and the South.
    • *the Civil War*
    • *the War between the States*
	The American Civil War is also known as the War between the States. It was a war between the people in the northern states and those in the southern states. Over the four-year period, more than 3 million Americans fought in the Civil War and more than 600,000 died.

74. Name one problem that led to the Civil War.
    • *slavery*
    • *economic reasons*
    • *states' rights*
	The Civil War lasted from 1861 to 1865. The problems that led to the Civil War were slavery, economic reasons and states' rights.

75. What was one important thing that Abraham Lincoln did?*
    • *freed the slaves (Emancipation Proclamation)*
    • *saved (or preserved) the Union*
    • *led the United States during the Civil War*
	Abraham Lincoln was president of the United States from 1861 to 1865 and led the nation during the Civil War.

76. What did the Emancipation Proclamation do? • *freed the slaves* • *freed slaves in the Confederacy* • *freed slaves in the Confederate states* • *freed slaves in most Southern states*	In 1863, in the middle of the Civil War, President Abraham Lincoln issued the Emancipation Proclamation. It declared that slaves living in the southern or Confederate states were free. The Emancipation Proclamation led to the 13th Amendment to the Constitution, which ended slavery in all of the United States.
77. What did Susan B. Anthony do? • *fought for women's rights* • *fought for civil rights*	Susan B. Anthony was born in Massachusetts on February 15, 1820. She is known for campaigning for the right of women to vote. In 1979, she became the first woman whose image appeared on a U.S. coin., the Susan B. Anthony dollar.
78. Name one war fought by the United States in the 1900s.* • *World War I* • *World War II* • *Korean War* • *Vietnam War* • *(Persian) Gulf War*	The United States fought five wars in the 1900s: World War I, World War II, the Korean War, the Vietnam War, and the (Persian) Gulf War.

79. Who was President during World War I? • *(Woodrow) Wilson*	Woodrow Wilson was the 28th president of the United States. President Wilson served two terms from 1913 to 1921.
80. Who was President during the Great Depression and World War II? • *(Franklin) Roosevelt*	Franklin Delano Roosevelt (FDR) was president of the United States from 1933 until 1945. Roosevelt led the nation into World War II after Japan's attack on Pearl Harbor in December 1941
81. Who did the United States fight in World War II? • *Japan, Germany, and Italy*	The Japanese bombed U.S. naval bases in a surprise attack on Pearl Harbor, Hawaii, on December 7, 1941. The next day, President Franklin D. Roosevelt obtained an official declaration of war from Congress. Japan's partners in the Axis, Italy and Germany. The Allies fought against the German Nazis, the Italian Fascists, and Japan's military empire.

82. Before he was President, Eisenhower was a general. What war was he in? • *World War II*	Before becoming the 34th president of the United States in 1953, Dwight D. Eisenhower served as a major general in World War II. Eisenhower left the White House in 1961, after serving two terms as president.
83. During the Cold War, what was the main concern of the United States? • *Communism*	The main concern of the United States during the Cold War was the spread of communism. The Cold War began shortly after the end of World War II and lasted for more than 40 years. It ended with the fall of the Berlin Wall in 1989, the reunification of East and West Germany in 1990, and the breakup of the USSR in 1991.
84. What movement tried to end racial discrimination? • *civil rights (movement)*	The goal of the civil rights movement was to end racial discrimination against African Americans and to gain full and equal rights for Americans of all.

85. What did Martin Luther King, Jr. do?* • *fought for civil rights* • *worked for equality for all Americans*	Martin Luther King, Jr. worked hard to make America a more fair, tolerant, and equal nation. He was the main leader of the civil rights movement of the 1950s and 1960s. He received the Nobel Peace Prize in 1964.
86. What major event happened on Sept. 11, 2001, in the United States? • *Terrorists attacked the United States.*	On September 11, 2001, four airplanes flying out of U.S. airports were taken over by terrorists from the Al-Qaeda network of Islamic extremists. Two of the planes crashed into the World Trade Center's Twin Towers in New York City. One of the planes crashed into the Pentagon in Arlington, Virginia. The fourth plane, originally aimed at Washington, D.C., crashed in a field in Pennsylvania.

87. Name one American Indian tribe in the United States.
- Cherokee
- Navajo
- Sioux
- Chippewa
- Choctaw
- Pueblo
- Apache
- Iroquois
- Creek
- Blackfeet
- Seminole
- Inuit
- Cheyenne
- Arawak
- Shawnee
- Mohegan
- Huron
- Oneida
- Lakota
- Crow
- Hopi
- Teton

American Indians lived in North America for thousands of years before the European settlers arrived. Today there are more than 500 federally recognized as tribes in the United States.

The federal government signed treaties with American Indian tribes to move the tribes to reservations. These reservations are recognized as domestic, dependent nations.

88. Name one of the two longest rivers in the United States.
- *Missouri (River)*
- *Mississippi (River)*

The Mississippi River is one of America's longest rivers
It runs through 10 U.S. states.
The Mississippi River was used by American Indians for trade, food, and water before Europeans came to America.

89. What ocean is on the West Coast of the United States? • *Pacific (Ocean)*	The Pacific Ocean is on the West Coast of the United States. It is the largest ocean on Earth and covers one-third of the Earth's surface.
90. What ocean is on the East Coast of the United States? • *Atlantic (Ocean)*	The Atlantic Ocean is on the East Coast of the United States. It is the second largest ocean in the world.

91. Name one U.S. territory.
   • *Puerto Rico*
   • *U.S. Virgin Islands*
   • *American Samoa*
   • *Northern Mariana Islands*
   • *Guam*
	A U.S. territory is a partially self-governing piece of land under the authority of the U.S. government.
	U.S. territories are not states.
	They do have representation in Congress.
	Each territory is allowed to send a delegate to the House of Representatives.

92. Name one state that borders Canada. • *Maine* • *Minnesota* • *New Hampshire* • *North Dakota* • *Vermont* • *Montana* • *New York* • *Idaho* • *Pennsylvania* • *Washington* • *Ohio* • *Alaska* • *Michigan*	The northern border of the United States stretches more than 5,000 miles from Maine in the East to Alaska in the West. There are 13 states on the border with Canada
93. Name one state that borders Mexico. • *California* • *Arizona* • *New Mexico* • *Texas*	The border between the United States and Mexico is about 1,900 miles long and spans four U.S. states - Arizona, California, New Mexico, and Texas.
94. What is the capital of the United States?* • *Washington, D.C.*	George Washington chose a location for the capital along the Potomac River between Maryland and Virginia. The capital is now known as Washington, D.C. (D.C. is the abbreviation for "District of Columbia".)

95. Where is the Statue of Liberty?* • *New York (Harbor)* • *Liberty Island* • *New Jersey* • *near New York City* • *on the Hudson (River)*	The Statue of Liberty is on Liberty Island, a 12-acre island in the New York harbor.
96. Why does the flag have 13 stripes? • *because there were 13 original colonies* • *because the stripes represent the original colonies*	There are 13 stripes on the flag because there were 13 original colonies. We call the American flag "the Stars and Stripes." In 1818, Congress decided that the number of stripes on the flag should always be 13.
97. Why does the flag have 50 stars?* • *because there is one star for each state* • *because each star represents a state* • *because there are 50 states*	Each star on the flag represents a state. This is why the number of stars has changed over the years from 13 to 50.

98. What is the name of the national anthem? ● *The Star-Spangled Banner*	During the War of 1812, Francis Scott Key watched the bombing of a fort and thought that the fort would fall. As the sun rose the next morning, Key looked toward the fort. He saw that the flag above the fort was still flying. Key immediately wrote the words to a poem which later became "The Star-Spangled Banner."
99. When do we celebrate Independence Day?* ● *July 4*	In the United States, we celebrate Independence Day on July 4 to mark the anniversary of the adoption of the Declaration of Independence.

100. Name two national U.S. holidays.
    ● *New Year's Day*
    ● *Columbus Day*
    ● *Martin Luther King, Jr. Day*
    ● *Veterans Day*
    ● *Presidents' Day*
    ● *Thanksgiving*
    ● *Memorial Day*
    ● *Christmas*
    ● *Independence Day*
    ● *Juneteenth National Independence Day*
	These holidays are "national" in a legal sense only for federal institutions and in the District of Columbia. Typically, federal offices are closed on these holidays.

100 Civics Q&A Practice	100 Official Civics Questions and Answer in Quiz style so you can test your memory of the questions and easy answers

Study Suggestion

There are as many ways to study as there are people.

One way to remember things is the repetition method, especially when we break up the studying into small fragments and over a long period of time.

Some experts suggest that you should wait a little longer each time before you review.

They discovered that when we spread out our studying over time, we remember things better.

This applies very much to learning and remembering the civics questions and answers. By repeated review, you will remember better and save time!

———————

CITIZENSHIP TEST PREP

(Cover the answers when practicing the civics questions.)

CITIZENSHIP TEST PREP

1. What is the supreme law of the land?	
2. What does the Constitution do?	
3. The idea of self-government is in the first three words of the Constitution. What are these words?	
4. What is an amendment?	
5. What do we call the first ten amendments to the Constitution?	
6. What is one right or freedom from the First Amendment?*	
7. How many amendments does the Constitution have?	

8. What did the Declaration of Independence do?	• *announced our indepen*
	  Great Britain)
	• *declared our independence (fr*
	  Great Britain)
	• *said that the United States is free*

1. What is the supreme law of the land?	• *the Constitution*
2. What does the Constitution do?	• *sets up the government* • *defines the government* • *protects basic rights of Americans*
3. The idea of self-government is in the first three words of the Constitution. What are these words?	• *We the People*
4. What is an amendment?	• *a change (to the Constitution)* • *an addition (to the Constitution)*
5. What do we call the first ten amendments to the Constitution?	• *the Bill of Rights*
6. What is one right or freedom from the First Amendment?*	• *Speech* • *religion* • *assembly* • *press* • *petition the government*
7. How many amendments does the Constitution have?	• *twenty-seven (27)*

8. What did the Declaration of Independence do?	• *announced our independence (from Great Britain)* • *declared our independence (from Great Britain)* • *said that the United States is free (from Great Britain)*
9. What are two rights in the Declaration of Independence?	• *Life* • *liberty* • *pursuit of happiness*
10. What is freedom of religion?	• *You can practice any religion, or not practice a religion.*
11. What is the economic system in the United States?*	• *capitalist economy* • *market economy*
12. What is the "rule of law"?	• *Everyone must follow the law.* • *Leaders must obey the law.* • *Government must obey the law.* • *No one is above the law.*
13. Name one branch or part of the government.*	• *Congress (legislative)* • *President (executive)* • *the courts (judicial)*
14. What stops one branch of government from becoming too powerful?	• *checks and balances* • *separation of powers*
15. Who is in charge of the executive branch?	• *the President*

16. Who makes federal laws?	• *Congress* • *Senate and House (of representatives)* • *(U.S. or national) Legislature*
17. What are the two parts of the U.S. Congress?*	• *Senate and House (of Representatives)*
18. How many U.S. Senators are there?	• one hundred (100)
19. We elect a U.S. Senator for how many years?	• *six (6)*
20. Who is one of your state's U.S. Senators now?*	• *Answers depends upon which state you live in*
21. The House of Representatives has how many voting members?	• *four hundred thirty-five (435)*
22. We elect a U.S. Representative for how many years?	• *two (2)*
23. Name your U.S. Representative.	• *Answers depend on where you live.*
24. Who does a U.S. Senator represent?	• *all people of the state*
25. Why do some states have more Representatives than other states?	• *(because of) the state's population* • *(because) they have more people* • *(because) some states have more people*

26. We elect a President for how many years?	● *four (4)*
27. In what month do we vote for President?*	● *November*
28. What is the name of the President of the United States now?*	● *Visit uscis.gov/citizenship/testupdates for the name of the President of the United States.*
29. What is the name of the Vice President of the United States now?	● *Visit uscis.gov/citizenship/testupdates for the name of the Vice President of the United States.*
30. If the President can no longer serve, who becomes President?	● *the Vice President*
31. If both the President and the Vice President can no longer serve, who becomes President?	● *the Speaker of the House*
32. Who is the Commander in Chief of the military?	● *the President*
33. Who signs bills to become laws?	● *the President*
34. Who vetoes bills?	● *the President*
35. What does the President's Cabinet do?	● *advises the President*

36. What are two Cabinet-level positions?	• *Secretary of Agriculture* • *Secretary of Transportation* • *Secretary of Commerce* • *Secretary of Veterans Affairs* • *Secretary of Defense* • *Secretary of the Treasury* • *Secretary of Education* • *Secretary of the Interior* • *Secretary of Energy* • *Secretary of Labor* • *Secretary of Health and Human Services* • *Secretary of State* • *Secretary of Homeland Security* • *Attorney General* • *Secretary of Housing and Urban Development* • *Vice President*
37. What does the judicial branch do?	• *reviews laws* • *explains laws* • *resolves disputes (disagreements)* • *decides if a law goes against the Constitution*
38. What is the highest court in the United States?	• *the Supreme Court*
39. How many justices are on the Supreme Court?	• *nine (9)*

40. Who is the Chief Justice of the United States now?	• *Visit uscis.gov/citizenship/testupdates for the name of the Chief Justice of the United States*
41. Under our Constitution, some powers belong to the federal government. What is one power of the federal government?	• *to print money* • *to declare war* • *to create an army* • *to make treaties*
42. Under our Constitution, some powers belong to the states. What is one power of the states?	• *provide schooling and education* • *provide protection (police, provide safety, fire departments)* • *give a driver's license* • *approve zoning and land use*
43. Who is the Governor of your state now?	• *Answers will vary. (District of Columbia residents should answer that D.C. does not have a Governor.) Visit usa.gov/states-and-territories to find the Governor of your state.*
44. What is the capital of your state?*	• *Answers vary. (District of Columbia residents should answer that D.C. is not a state and does not have a capital. Residents of U.S. territories should name the capital of the territory.)*

45. What are the two major political parties in the United States?*	• *Democratic and Republican*
46. What is the political party of the President now?	• *Visit uscis.gov/citizenship/testupdates for the political party of the President.*
47. What is the name of the Speaker of the House of Representatives now?	• *Visit uscis.gov/citizenship/testupdates for the name of the Speaker of the House of Representatives.*
48. There are four amendments to the Constitution about who can vote. Describe one of them.	• *Citizens eighteen (18) and older (can vote).* • *You don't have to pay (a poll tax) to vote.* • *Any citizen can vote. (Women and men can vote.)* • *A male citizen of any race (can vote).*
49. What is one responsibility that is only for United States citizens?*	• *serve on a jury* • *vote in a federal election*
50. Name one right only for United States citizens.	• *vote in a federal election* • *run for federal office*
51. What are two rights of everyone living in the United States?	• *freedom of expression* • *freedom to petition the government* • *freedom of speech* • *freedom of worship* • *freedom of assembly* • *the right to bear arms*

52. What do we show loyalty to when we say the Pledge of Allegiance?	• *the United States* • *the flag*
53. What is one promise you make when you become a United States citizen?	• *give up loyalty to other countries* • *defend the Constitution and laws of the United States* • *obey the laws of the United States* • *serve in the U.S. military (if needed)* • *serve (do important work for) the nation (if needed)* • *be loyal to the United States*
54. How old do citizens have to be to vote for President?*	• *eighteen (18) and older*
55. What are two ways that Americans can participate in their democracy?	• *vote* • *join a political party* • *help with a campaign* • *join a civic group* • *join a community group* • *give an elected official your opinion on an issue* • *call Senators and Representatives* • *publicly support or oppose an issue or policy* • *run for office* • *write to a newspaper*
56. When is the last day you can send in federal income tax forms?*	• *April 15*

57. When must all men register for the Selective Service?	• *at age eighteen (18)* • *between eighteen (18) and twenty-six (26)*
58. What is one reason colonists came to America?	• *freedom* • *political liberty* • *religious freedom* • *economic opportunity* • *practice their religion* • *escape persecution*
59. Who lived in America before the Europeans arrived?	• *American Indians* • *Native Americans*
60. What group of people was taken to America and sold as slaves?	• *Africans* • *people from Africa*
61. Why did the colonists fight the British?	• *because of high taxes (taxation without representation)* • *because the British army stayed in their houses (boarding, quartering)* • *because they didn't have self-Government*
62. Who wrote the Declaration of Independence?	• *(Thomas) Jefferson*
63. When was the Declaration of Independence adopted?	• *July 4, 1776*

64. There were 13 original states. Name three.	• *New Hampshire* • *Delaware* • *Massachusetts* • *Maryland* • *Rhode Island* • *Virginia* • *Connecticut* • *North Carolina* • *New York* • *South Carolina* • *New Jersey* • *Georgia* • *Pennsylvania*
65. What happened at the Constitutional Convention?	• *The Constitution was written.* • *The Founding Fathers wrote the Constitution.*
66. When was the Constitution written?	• *1787*
67. The Federalist Papers supported the passage of the U.S. Constitution. Name one of the writers.	• *(James) Madison* • *(Alexander) Hamilton* • *(John) Jay* • *Publius*
68. What is one thing Benjamin Franklin is famous for?	• *U.S. diplomat* • *oldest member of the Constitutional Convention* • *first Postmaster General of the United States* • *writer of "Poor Richard's Almanac"* • *started the first free libraries*

69. Who is the "Father of Our Country"?	• *(George) Washington*
70. Who was the first President?*	• *(George) Washington*
71. What territory did the United States buy from France in 1803?	• *the Louisiana Territory* • *Louisiana*
72. Name one war fought by the United States in the 1800s.	• *War of 1812* • *Mexican-American War* • *Civil War* • *Spanish-American War*
73. Name the U.S. war between the North and the South.	• *the Civil War* • *the War between the States*
74. Name one problem that led to the Civil War.	• *slavery* • *economic reasons* • *states' rights*
75. What was one important thing that Abraham Lincoln did?*	• *freed the slaves (Emancipation Proclamation)* • *saved (or preserved) the Union* • *led the United States during the Civil War*
76. What did the Emancipation Proclamation do?	• *freed the slaves* • *freed slaves in the Confederacy* • *freed slaves in the Confederate states* • *freed slaves in most Southern States*

77. What did Susan B. Anthony do?	• *fought for women's rights* • *fought for civil rights*
78. Name one war fought by the United States in the 1900s.*	• *World War I* • *World War II* • *Korean War* • *Vietnam War* • *(Persian) Gulf War*
79. Who was President during World War I?	• *(Woodrow) Wilson*
80. Who was President during the Great Depression and World War II?	• *(Franklin) Roosevelt*
81. Who did the United States fight in World War II?	• *Japan, Germany, and Italy*
82. Before he was President, Eisenhower was a general. What war was he in?	• *World War II*
83. During the Cold War, what was the main concern of the United States?	• *Communism*
84. What movement tried to end racial discrimination?	• *civil rights (movement)*

85. What did Martin Luther King, Jr. do?*	• *fought for civil rights* • *worked for equality for all Americans*
86. What major event happened on Sept. 11, 2001, in the United States?	• *Terrorists attacked the United States.*
87. Name one American Indian tribe in the United States.	• Cherokee • Navajo • Sioux • Chippewa • Choctaw • Pueblo • Apache • Iroquois • Creek • Blackfeet • Seminole • Inuit • Cheyenne • Arawak • Shawnee • Mohegan • Huron • Oneida • Lakota • Crow • Hopi • Teton
88. Name one of the two longest rivers in the United States.	• *Missouri (River)* • *Mississippi (River)*

89. What ocean is on the West Coast of the United States?	• *Pacific (Ocean)*
90. What ocean is on the East Coast of the United States?	• *Atlantic (Ocean)*
91. Name one U.S. territory.	• *Puerto Rico* • *U.S. Virgin Islands* • *American Samoa* • *Northern Mariana Islands* • *Guam*
92. Name one state that borders Canada.	• *Maine* • *Minnesota* • *New Hampshire* • *North Dakota* • *Vermont* • *Montana* • *New York* • *Idaho* • *Pennsylvania* • *Washington* • *Ohio* • *Alaska* • *Michigan*
93. Name one state that borders Mexico.	• *California* • *Arizona* • *New Mexico* • *Texas*

94. What is the capital of the United States?*	• *Washington, D.C.*
95. Where is the Statue of Liberty?*	• *New York (Harbor)* • *Liberty Island* • *New Jersey* • *near New York City* • *on the Hudson (River)*
96. Why does the flag have 13 stripes?	• *because there were 13 original colonies* • *because the stripes represent the original colonies*
97. Why does the flag have 50 stars?*	• *because there is one star for each state* • *because each star represents a state* • *because there are 50 states*
98. What is the name of the national anthem?	• *The Star-Spangled Banner*
99. When do we celebrate Independence Day?*	• *July 4*

100. Name two national U.S. holidays.	• *New Year's Day* • *Columbus Day* • *Martin Luther King, Jr. Day* • *Veterans Day* • *Presidents' Day* • *Thanksgiving* • *Memorial Day* • *Christmas* • *Independence Day* • *Juneteenth National Independence Day*

Writing Words	All the writing words (vocabulary) you need to know how to write, including practice sentences

People	Civics	Places	Months
Adams	American Indians	Alaska	February
Lincoln	capital	California	May
Washington	citizens	Canada	June
	Civil War	Delaware	July
	Congress	Mexico	September
	Father of Our Country	New York City	October
	flag	United States	November
	free	Washington	
	freedom of speech	Washington, D.C.	
	President		
	Right		
	Senators		
	State / states		
	White House		

Verbs	Holidays	— Other —		
can	Presidents' Day	and	blue	
come	Memorial Day	during	dollar bill	
elect	Flag Day	for	fifty / 50	
have/has	Independence Day	here	first	
is / was / be	Labor Day	in	largest	
lives / lived	Columbus Day	of	most	
meets	Thanksgiving	on	north	
pay		the	one	
vote		to	one hundred /100	
want		we	people	
			red	
			second	
			south	
			taxes	
			white	

CITIZENSHIP TEST PREP

Writing Words Practice

The number of words on the official "Writing Vocabulary for the Naturalization Test" is less than 100.

For applicants who speak and write English, this part of the test is relatively easy.

However, if your native language does not have the 26 letters of the English alphabet, or you are not yet proficient in speaking English, this part of the test may require some concentration and practice.

We suggest that you first practice the individual words and phrases. After you have practiced writing them, have a friend or relative (or our citizenship app) pronounce the word or phrase, and then write it on a piece of better (or better, write it with a stylus on a tablet, as that is the way you will take the written test at the Naturalization Interview).

Compare your written word with the word on the official list of words. Did you hear the word correctly? Did you write it correctly? We suggest that you practice listening to the word and writing it repeatedly until you get it right. Many people like to print the word (instead of writing it in script letters) as that makes it easier for them to write the word in English.

There is a saying that "Practice Makes Perfect."

Practice, Practice, Practice until you get it just right!

———————

CITIZENSHIP TEST PREP

Writing Sentences Practice

The following sentences contain all the words that you need to know how to <u>write</u>. Have a friend or relative read each sentence to you, and then write the sentence. Check to see if you spelled each word correctly.

As with everything else, the more you practice, the better you will do.

_____

1. We pay taxes.

2. The flag is here.

3. Citizens can vote.

4. People can be free.

5. Alaska is a state.

6. Pay for the flag.

7. We want to vote.

8. Citizens pay taxes.

9. We lived in Canada.

10. Pay here for the flag.

11. Most people can vote.

12. Flag Day is in June.

13. Pay for the largest flag.

14. The largest flag is free.

15. Senators vote for taxes.

16. One state is Delaware.

17. People want to be free.

18. Adams was President

19. Washington is one State.

20. The Senators vote here.

21. Citizens elect the Senators.

22. Alaska is the largest state.

23. Alaska is north of Mexico.

24. Mexico is south of Canada.

25. Memorial Day is in May.

26. Independence Day is in July.

27. Labor Day is in September.

28. Columbus Day is in October.

29. The Senators want to vote.

30. The White House is white.

31. Delaware is north of Mexico.

32. Citizens vote in November.

33. Come to the White House.

34. Is Canada the largest state?

35. American Indians can vote.

36. One Right is the right to vote.

37. The largest state is Alaska.

38. Thanksgiving is in November.

39. Citizens elect the President.

40. We the citizens elect Congress.

41. The White House is here.

42. American Indians in Alaska vote.

43. The second President was Adams.

44. The right to vote is one right.

45. Citizens want freedom of speech.

46. The President meets the people.

47. The White House is in the capital.

48. United States citizens pay taxes.

49. Is Washington, D.C. in Washington?

50. Congress meets in Washington, D.C.

51. California has the most people.

52. Presidents day is in February.

53. Washington is on the dollar bill.

54. Unites States citizens can vote.

55. Lincoln lived in the White House.

56. The flag is red, white and blue.

57. American Indians lived in Alaska.

58. Freedom of speech is one Right.

59. California is south of Washington.

60. The President lives in Washington, D.C.

61. New York City has the most people.

62. Adams was the second President.

63. One Right is freedom of speech.

64. Freedom of speech is one Right.

65. Washington was the first President.

66. The first President was Washington.

67. The people lived in Washington.

68. People come during Thanksgiving.

69. We can come to the White House.

70. Canada is north of the United States.

71. Mexico is south of the United States.

72. Delaware is south of New York City.

73. New York City is in the United States.

74. Come during Independence Day.

75. Most people have one dollar bill.

76. New York City is the largest one.

77. New York City is north of Delaware.

78. The White House is in Washington, D.C.

79. The United States has fifty (50) states.

80. The President lives in the White House.

81. Washington is the Father of Our Country.

82. People come here for freedom of speech.

83. Congress has one hundred (100) Senators.

84. The White House has the largest flag.

85. We have the Right of freedom of speech.

86. The Father of Our Country is Washington.

87. Lincoln was President during the Civil War.

88. Alaska is the largest of the 50 (fifty) states.

89. People come to the United States to be free.

90. People want American Indians to vote.

91. The President meets people at the White House.

92. Citizens elect the President and the Senators.

93. The President and the Senators pay taxes.

94. During the Civil War the President was Lincoln.

95. American Indians lived first in the United States.

96. The capital of the United States is Washington, D.C.

97. American Indians lived in the United States first.

98. One President lived in Washington D.C. and New York City.

99. Presidents' Day and Memorial Day come before Thanksgiving.

100. The one hundred (100) Senators vote in Washington, D.C.

Reading Words	All the reading words (vocabulary) you need to know how to read, including practice sentences

People	Civics	Places	Holidays
Abraham Lincoln George Washington	American flag Bill of Rights capital citizen city Congress country Father of Our Country government President right senators state / states White House	America U.S. United States	Presidents' Day Memorial Day Flag Day Independence Day Labor Day Columbus Day Thanksgiving

Question Words	Verbs	Other	
How What When Where Who Why	can come do/does elects have / has is / are / was / be lives / lived meet name pay vote want	a for here in of on the to we	colors dollar bill first largest many most north one people second south

CITIZENSHIP TEST PREP

Reading Sentences Practice
The following are 100 sentences for you to practice reading the words. They contain all the words that you must know how to read.
Have a friend or relative read a sentence, and then you read the sentence. Have the friend or relative tell you if you are reading the sentence correctly.
Remember, the more you practice, the better you will do.

1. Pay here.

2. We want to pay.

3. We want to vote.

4. What is Flag Day?

5. Why be the first?

6. When is Labor Day?

7. Be first to vote.

8. Where is the south?

9. Where do we pay?

10. The senators are here.

11. When do people vote?

12. Where is the north?

13. Who elects Congress?

14. When is Memorial Day?

15. When does one vote?

16. What is Thanksgiving?

17. What is the Congress?

18. We lived in the south.

19. When does Flag Day come?

20. Who can be a citizen?

21. Why do people vote?

22. America is in the north.

23. The capital is a city.

24. When is Independence Day?

25. America is a country.

26. When is Presidents' Day?

27. Where is the largest city?

28. The President was here.

29. When do the people vote?

30. We can meet the President.

31. Most senators are here.

32. We can meet the Senators.

33. We want to do what is right.

34. The largest city is here.

35. Who was Abraham Lincoln?

36. The White House is here.

37. Come here on Labor Day.

38. Where is the dollar bill?

39. Who elects the U.S. senators?

40. How does a citizen vote?

41. Where is the White House?

42. When is Independence Day?

43. The capital is in the north.

44. Name a state in the south.

45. Abraham Lincoln lived here.

46. The south has many people.

47. People lived in many states.

48. Who was George Washington?

49. Who is the first citizen?

50. A citizen has to vote here.

51. Was Abraham Lincoln a President?

52. Where do we meet the senators?

53. What is the Bill of Rights?

54. Name one right of a citizen.

55. Who lives in the White House?

56. People come in many colors.

57. What is the largest state?

58. Why do people want to vote?

59. Most states are in the north.

60. What is the largest country?

61. Senators meet in the capital.

62. The north has the most people.

63. The American flag has colors.

64. Who was the second President?

65. The people elect the Congress.

66. Abraham Lincoln was a President.

67. George Washington lived here.

68. Many states are in the south.

69. The United States is a country.

70. What is the Bill of Rights?

71. Many people lived in the south.

72. The government has many senators.

73. What country is south of the U.S.?

74. Who is the Father of Our Country?

75. Senators meet in the capital city.

76. The largest state is in the north.

77. The second name is Abraham Lincoln.

78. The government is for the people.

79. How many rights do citizens have?

80. What country is north of the U.S.?

81. How many Senators are in Congress?

82. What is the name of the President?

83. Abraham Lincoln lived in the north.

84. Where is the capital of the country?

85. The President is the first citizen.

86. When are Columbus Day and Thanksgiving?

87. United States people have many rights.

88. The President lives in the White House.

89. George Washington is on the dollar bill.

90. George Washington was the first President.

91. Presidents' Day and Memorial Day come first.

92. The second President lived in the south.

93. The capital of the United States is a city.

94. How many colors does the American flag have?

95. Citizens vote for the government of America.

96. Why is George Washington on the dollar bill?

97. Abraham Lincoln was a United States President.

98. What is the name of the Father of Our Country?

99. The father of our country is George Washington.

100. Where is the largest city in the United States?

Citizenship Interview	Step by step explanation and practice for the citizenship (Naturalization) interview

To be approved for citizenship, a person must pass a citizenship (naturalization) interview with a USCIS (U.S. Citizenship and Immigration Services) officer.

What are some things that happen at the naturalization (citizenship) interview?

> You can see the official **FREE USCIS video** which has an example of the interview. The video is excellent and has earned high praises from many people.
>
> **The link to the official website is on page 107 of this book.**

Among the things you should take to the interview are:

1. Copy of your N-400 Application (Review it carefully so that you are able to answer questions about it.)
2. Letter with interview appointment notice.

Interview Process

At the interview, the Naturalization (Citizenship) officer will place you under oath.

You will stand up and raise your right hand and promise to tell the truth during the interview.

The following is one version of the oath:

"Do you swear (or affirm) that the statements you will give today will be the truth, the whole truth, and nothing but the truth?

At the end of the oath, you will say, "I do."

The officer will also check your identity.

You will show your ID cards (like your Green Card, passport, and driver's license.)

(Make sure these documents are current and not expired.)

The officer will review with you the N-400 Application for Naturalization) which you filled out and ask questions and review any documents you submitted.

The officer will check your name, address, job, travel, and if you are married.

Here are some possible questions and possible answers:

What is your name?

> Maria Elena Ortiz

Where do you live?

> 2835 Everyday Drive, Franklin, California

Do you work?

> "Yes" or "No."

Where do you work?

> "Seaside Fusion Restaurant"

Have you travelled outside the United States in the last five years?

> "Yes" or "No."

The officer will ask you some background questions, such as:

"Have you ever been arrested?"

> "Yes" or "No."

If you become a citizen, will you be loyal to the United States?

> "Yes."

The officer will use this to review your ability to speak and understand the English language.

While talking with the officer, they will see how well you can speak English.
If at any time you don't hear or don't understand a question, ask the officer to repeat the question.: "Can you please repeat that?"

Tips
Speak clearly and confidently
Take your time to understand each question.
Don't be afraid to ask for clarification.
Answer in complete sentences when possible.

CITIZENSHIP TEST PREP

Here is a more extensive list of questions that might be asked:

1. What is your full legal name?
2. Have you used any other names since birth?
3. What is your date of birth?
4. In which country were you born?
5. Are you a citizen of any other country?
6. What is your current home address?
7. How long have you lived at your current address?
8. What was your previous address?
9. What is your phone number?
10. What is your current occupation or job?
11. Where do you work?
12. Have you traveled outside the United States in the last five years?
13. Can you provide details about your trips outside the U.S.?
14. Are you married, single, divorced, or widowed?
15. What is your spouse's name?
16. Is your spouse a U.S. citizen?
17. Do you have any children?
18. What are your children's names and dates of birth?
19. Have you ever claimed to be a U.S. citizen in the past?
20. Have you ever registered to vote or voted in the United States?
21. Do you owe any overdue federal, state, or local taxes?
22. Have you ever not filed a required tax return?
23. Have you ever been a member of any club or organization?
24. Have you ever been arrested, cited, or detained by any law enforcement officer?
25. Have you ever been charged with committing any crime or offense?
26. Have you ever been convicted of a crime or offense?
27. Have you ever given false or misleading information to a U.S. government official?
28. Have you ever lied to obtain public benefits in the United States?
29. Do you support the Constitution and form of government of the United States?
30. Are you willing to take the full Oath of Allegiance to the United States?

CITIZENSHIP TEST PREP

U.S. Naturalization Interview Practice Form

Practice Instructions:

For each of the following questions, write your answer honestly and accurately. This will help you prepare for the kinds of questions you might be asked during your interview.

Practice speaking your answers out loud. This will help you become more comfortable with the language and the information.

Review your answers regularly. Familiarize yourself with your personal information and with each answer so that at the interview you will answer confidently.

Seek professional or legal help if needed. If you're unsure about any questions or how to answer them, consider consulting an immigration attorney or a trusted advisor.

Note: During the actual interview, always answer truthfully. Providing false information can have serious consequences for your naturalization application.

---

1. What is your full legal name?

Answer: _____

2. Have you used any other names since birth?

Answer: _____

3. What is your date of birth?

Answer: _____

4. In which country were you born?

Answer: _____

5. Are you a citizen of any other country?

Answer: _____

6. What is your current home address?

Answer: _____

7. How long have you lived at your current address?

Answer: _____

8. What was your previous address?

Answer: _____

9. What is your phone number?

Answer: _____

10. What is your current occupation or job?

Answer: _____

11. Where do you work?

Answer: _____

12. Have you traveled outside the United States in the last five years?

Answer: _____

13. Can you provide details about your trips outside the U.S.?

Answer: _____

14. Are you married, single, divorced, or widowed?

Answer: _____

15. What is your spouse's name?

Answer: _____

16. Is your spouse a U.S. citizen?

Answer: _____

17. Do you have any children?

Answer: _____

18. What are your children's names and dates of birth?

Answer: _____

19. Have you ever claimed to be a U.S. citizen in the past?

Answer: _____

20. Have you ever registered to vote or voted in the United States?

Answer: _____

21. Do you owe any overdue federal, state, or local taxes?

Answer: _____

22. Have you ever not filed a required tax return?

Answer: _____

23. Have you ever been a member of any club or organization?

Answer: _____

24. Have you ever been arrested, cited, or detained by any law enforcement officer?

Answer: _____

25. Have you ever been charged with committing any crime or offense?

Answer: _____

26. Have you ever been convicted of a crime or offense?

Answer: _____

27. Have you ever given false or misleading information to a U.S. government official?

Answer: _____

28. Have you ever lied to obtain public benefits in the United States?

Answer: _____

29. Do you support the Constitution and form of government of the United States?

Answer: _____

30. Are you willing to take the full Oath of Allegiance to the United States?

Answer: _____

_____

CITIZENSHIP TEST PREP

During the interview (either before or after reviewing the N-400 form) the officer will ask civics questions and test your reading and writing ability.

1. The officer may ask up to 10 civics questions.

The questions are asked orally by the officer and you answer orally.

To pass the test, you must answer at least 6 of the questions correctly.

(Once you have reached 6 correct answers, the officer will stop asking you civics questions.)

2. For the reading test, the officer will ask you to read up to three simple sentences displayed on a digital tablet. You must read at least one sentence correctly to pass.

3. For the writing test, the officer will say up to three sentences.

You must write at least one sentence correctly on a digital tablet to pass.

At the end of the test, the officer will tell you if you passed or not.

After you pass, you will be scheduled for the citizenship oath ceremony, which is the final step in the naturalization (citizenship) process.

Congratulations!

Studying for the Three Parts of the Citizenship Test

Part 1. Civics Questions (History, Government and Geography)

At the citizenship interview you will be asked up to 10 questions from the official 100 questions that the government has provided.

All 100 questions and answers are included in this book - in ways that will help you remember them fast!

To pass the civics part of the test, you must answer correctly at least 6 questions out of 10. Some of the questions have more than one acceptable answer (For each question, we suggest what we believe is the easiest answer for you to memorize.)

Note: Applicants who are 65 or older when they file the Application for Naturalization and who have been legal permanent residents of the United States for 20 or more years, may only need to study 20 questions and answers. We have marked these questions with a star * in this book.

Question numbers:
6, 11, 13, 17, 20, 27, 28, 44, 45, 49 54, 56, 70, 75, 78, 85, 94, 95, 97, 99

The other two parts of the citizenship test involve showing some basic ability in English reading and writing.

Part 2. English writing

During the citizenship interview, you will be asked to write on a tablet three (3) sentences containing specific words that the government has announced.

All the <u>writing</u> words (less than 100 words) are listed in this book and in our Writing Workbook.

To pass this writing section, you must write one sentence out of the three sentences in a manner that is understandable to the USCIS Officer.

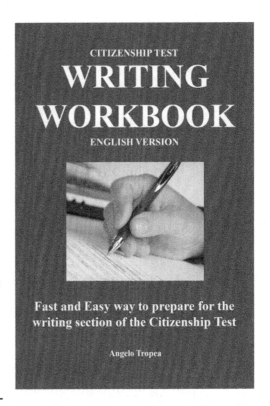

Part 3. English reading

You will be asked to read three (3) sentences displayed on a tablet containing specific words (less than 100) that the government has announced.

All the <u>reading</u> words (less than 100 words) are listed in this book and in our reading Workbook.

To pass this reading section, you must read one sentence out of the three sentences in a manner suggesting to the USCIS Officer that you appear to understand the meaning of the sentence.

A BRIEF HISTORY OF THE UNITED STATES

The aim of the following brief history of the United States is to help you put in a logical order many of the civics questions and answers. This will help you to understand and also remember them.

We suggest that at first you read the short history in a relaxed manner, without worrying about what you need to remember. After you have reviewed the questions and answers for some time, read the short history again. You will find that you will have greater understanding of both the questions and the history.

As one writer said, you need to stir your memory every now and then, as you would stir a sauce that you are preparing. Careful attention to studying and periodically "stirring" or "refreshing" your memory will go far in mastering the civics questions and answers.

100 CIVICS QUESTIONS

Grouped by U.S. History and categories

The following groups of civics questions are in a logical order which will make it easier for you to remember the Questions and Answers.

THE AMERICAN REVOLUTION
(FIGHT FOR FREEDOM)

Over many centuries, explorers from different places came to the "New World" (America). Christopher Columbus came to America (the New World) in 1492.

The people who lived in America before Europeans arrived were the American Indians, the native Americans. (Q.59)

The American Indians lived in many places and in different groups called tribes.

Indian Village

Some of the Indian tribes were the: Cherokee, Navajo, Sioux, Chippewa, Choctaw, Pueblo, Apache, Iroquois, Creek, Blackfeet, Seminole, Cheyenne, Arawak, Shawnee, Mohegan, Huron, Oneida, Lakota, Crow, Teton, Hopi, and Inuit. (Q.87)

In Europe in the 1500's and later years there were not many liberties or freedoms or economic opportunities. Because of this, it was difficult to live a good life.

People which we call "settlers" or "colonists" came to America. Some settled in South America, the Caribbean Islands, and some settled in North America—in what is now the United States and Canada.

Colonists came to America to get freedom, political liberty, economic opportunity, practice their religion, and escape persecution. (Q.58)

Some colonists from England (Great Britain) and other European countries settled in the eastern part of what is now the United States. At first, they lived in small villages and towns. As the population grew, they spread inland. Great Britain governed this area which we now refer to as the "thirteen colonies."

Newport Church

After the revolutionary war between the colonists and Great Britain, the thirteen colonies formed into the first 13 American states.

There were thirteen (13) original states. They are: New Hampshire, Massachusetts, Rhode Island, Connecticut, New York, New Jersey, Pennsylvania, Delaware, Maryland, Virginia, North Carolina, South Carolina, and Georgia. (Q.64)

On July 4, 1776, people from the thirteen states signed a paper called the Declaration of Independence.

The Declaration of Independence said that the 13 colonies were no longer colonies of England and that they were free and independent.

The Declaration of Independence was written by Thomas Jefferson. (Q.62)

Years later, Thomas Jefferson became a President of the United States.

The Declaration of Independence was adopted on July 4, 1776. (Q.63)

The Declaration of Independence: 1) announced our independence (from Great Britain), 2) declared our independence (from Great Britain), 3) said that the United States is free (from Great Britain). (Q.8)

Three rights stated in the Declaration of Independence are life, liberty, and the pursuit of happiness. (Q.9)

The colonists fought the British because of high taxes (taxation without representation) because the British army stayed in their houses (boarding, quartering), and because they didn't have self-government. (Q.61)

Boston Tea Party

Great Britain did not agree with the colonists trying to be independent.

The American Revolutionary war was a result of Great Britain trying to keep the colonies under its colonial control.

George Washington led the revolutionary army that fought against Great Britain. He also later became the first President of the United States. (Q.70)

The Father of Our Country is George Washington. (Q.69)

THE AMERICAN CONSTITUTION
(THE HIGHEST LAW OF THE U.S.)

In the United States, we agree that we must live by the rule of law. The "rule of law" means that everyone must follow the law, leaders must follow the law, and that no one is above the law. (Q.12)

In 1787 representatives from the 13 colonies wrote the constitution. Soon after that they added 10 changes to the constitution. These changes are called "amendments" to the constitution.

The Constitutional Convention

The Constitution was written in 1787. (Q.66)

At the Constitutional Convention, the constitution was written. The (founding fathers wrote the constitution). (Q.65)

The federalist papers (pamphlets that were printed for the people to read) supported the passage of the Constitution. The writers of the Federalist Papers were: (James) Madison, (Alexander) Hamilton, (John) Jay, and Publius. (Q.67)

Because there was disagreement as to what the Constitution should contain, some people proposed that the original Constitution should be changed or enlarged. They supported changes which we call "amendments" to the Constitution. An amendment is a change to the Constitution. (Q.4) An amendment is an addition to the Constitution. (Q.4)

We call the first ten amendments to the Constitution the "Bill of Rights." (Q. 5)

The constitution and the amendments say many things, including that all people have equal rights and that the government is elected by the people.

The Constitution is the supreme law of the land. (Q.1)

The Constitution sets up the government. (Q.2)

The Constitution defines the government. (Q.2)

The Constitution protects basic rights of Americans. (Q.2)

One freedom guaranteed by the Constitution is freedom of religion. Freedom of religion means that you can practice any religion, or not practice a religion. (Q.10)

The idea of self-government is in the first three words of the Constitution. These three words are "We the People." (Q.3)

The first amendment to the Constitution guarantees certain rights or freedoms.

The rights or freedoms in the First Amendment are: freedom of speech, freedom of religion, freedom of assembly (freedom to hold meetings), freedom of the press, and freedom to petition the government (ask the government to do something). (Q.6)

As the years passed, more amendments were added to the Constitution.

Today the Constitution has a total of twenty-seven (27) amendments. (Q.7)

Under the Constitution some powers belong to the federal government.

These powers are to print money, to declare war, to create an army, and to make treaties. (Q.41)

Under the Constitution some powers belong to the states. These powers are to provide schooling and education, provide protection (police), provide safety (fire departments), give a driver's license, and approve zoning and land use. (Q.42)

There are four amendments to the Constitution about who can vote: 1) citizens (18) and older can vote, 2) you don't have to pay a poll tax to vote, 3) any citizen, man or woman, can vote, and 4) a male citizen of any race can vote. (Q.48)

THE 3 BRANCHES OF GOVERNMENT
(THE STRUCTURE OF THE U.S. GOVERNMENT)

To make sure that no one person or agency has too much power, our government is divided into three (3) parts called "branches."

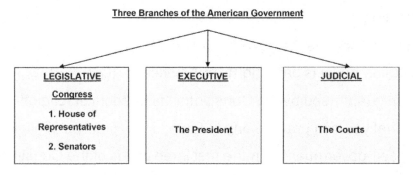

Three Branches of the American Government

The branches of our government are: Congress, legislative (President, executive), and the courts (judicial). (Q.13)

The checks and balances (separation of powers among the three branches) stop one branch of government from becoming too powerful. (Q.14)

The President is in charge of the executive branch of government. (Q.15)

The President is elected for four (4) years. (Q.26)

We elect the President in the month of November. (Q.27)

The President is Commander in Chief of the military. (Q.32)

The President signs bills to become laws. (Q.33)

The President can veto bills and stop them from becoming law. (Q.33)

The President appoints people to help him run the government. The top people become part of his cabinet.

CITIZENSHIP TEST PREP

The Cabinet

President's cabinet advises the President. (Q.35)

The following are Cabinet-level positions: Secretary of Agriculture, Secretary of Commerce, Secretary of Defense, Secretary of Education, Secretary of Energy, Secretary of Health and Human Services, Secretary of Homeland Security, Secretary of Housing and Urban Development, Secretary of the Interior, Secretary of Labor, Secretary of State, Secretary of Transportation, Secretary of The Treasury, Secretary of Veterans Affairs, Attorney General, and Vice President. (Q.36)

The name of the President of the United States now is _____ (Q.28)

The name of the Vice President now is _____. (Q.29)

If the President can no longer serve, the Vice President becomes President.(Q.30)

If both the President and the Vice President can no longer serve, the Speaker of the House becomes President. (Q.31)

The judicial branch: reviews laws, explains laws, resolves disputes (disagreements), and decides if a law goes against the Constitution. (Q.37) The highest court in the United States is the Supreme Court. (Q.38). There are nine (9) justices on the Supreme Court. (Q.39) The Chief Justice of the United States is _____. (Q.40)

The two parts of the U.S. Congress are the Senate and the House (of Representatives). (Q.17) Federal laws are made by Congress (Senate and House of Representatives), also known as the U.S. or national legislature). (Q.16)

There are one hundred (100) U.S. senators. (Q.18) U.S. Senators represent all the people of their state. (Q.24) U.S. Senators are elected for six (6) years. (Q.19)

The House of Representatives has 435 voting members. (Q.21) U.S. Representatives are elected for two (2) years. (Q.22) Some states have more Representatives than other states because of the state's population because they have more people, because some states have more people. (Q.25)

GEOGRAPHY OF THE U.S.

United States

(Q.88) Name one of the two longest rivers in the United States.

• Missouri (River)

• Mississippi (River)

(Q.89) What ocean is on the West Coast of the United States?

• Pacific (Ocean)

(Q.90) What ocean is on the East Coast of the United States?

• Atlantic (Ocean)

(Q.91) Name one U.S. territory.

• Puerto Rico, U.S. Virgin Islands, American Samoa, Northern Mariana, Islands, Guam

(Q.92) Name one state that borders Canada.

• Maine, Michigan, New Hampshire, Vermont, New York, Pennsylvania, Ohio, North Dakota, Minnesota, Montana, Idaho, Washington, Alaska

(Q.93) Name one state that borders Mexico.

• California, Arizona, New Mexico, Texas

(Q.94) What is the capital of the United States?

• Washington, D.C.

(Q.95) Where is the Statue of Liberty?

• New York (Harbor), Liberty Island, New Jersey, near New York City, and on the Hudson (River).

THE FLAG AND NATIONAL ANTHEM

American Flag

(Q.96) Why does the flag have 13 stripes?

• because there were 13 original colonies,

• because the stripes represent the original colonies

(Q.97) Why does the flag have 50 stars?

• because there is one star for each state, because each star represents a state, because there are 50 states

(Q.98) What is the name of the national anthem?

• The Star-Spangled Banner

FEDERAL HOLIDAYS

(Q.99) When do we celebrate Independence Day?

• July 4

Independence Day

(Q.100) Name two national U.S. holidays.

• New Year's Day, Columbus Day, Independence Day, Martin Luther King, Jr. Day, Veterans Day, Labor Day, Presidents' Day, Memorial Day, Thanksgiving, Christmas

MAJOR WARS

Problems that led to the Civil War were the following: slavery, economic reasons, and states' rights. (Q.74) The U.S. war between the North and the South is called the Civil War, or the War between the States. (Q.73) The Civil War lasted from 1861 to 1865. During the civil war, the President was Abraham Lincoln.

The Emancipation Proclamation was issued by President Lincoln. It freed the slaves, freed slaves in Confederate states, freed slaves in the Confederacy, freed slaves in most Southern states. (Q.76) President Abraham Lincoln: freed the slaves (Emancipation Proclamation), saved (or preserved) the Union, and led the United States during the Civil War. (Q.75)

CITIZENSHIP TEST PREP

In the 1800's the United States fought several wars: The War of 1812, the Mexican-American War, the Civil War, and the Spanish-American War. (Q.72)

In 1803 the United States bought from France the Louisiana Territory, also known as Louisiana. (Q.71). As the years passed, more states were added to the United States of America. Some states disagreed about such things as slavery. Africans (people from Africa) were taken to America and sold as slaves. (Q.60)

In the 1900's the United States fought several wars: World War I, World War II, Korean War, Vietnam War, and the (Persian) Gulf War. (Q.78)

During the First World War, the President was (Woodrow) Wilson. (Q.79)

During the Great Depression and World War II, the President was (Franklin) Roosevelt. (Q.80)

During World War II, the United States fought Japan, Italy, and Germany. (Q.81).

During World War II, Eisenhower was a general. (Q.82)

During the Cold War, the main concern of the U. S. was Communism. (Q.83)

On September 11, 2001, terrorists attacked the United States. (Q.86)

CITIZENSHIP TEST PREP

YOUR POLITICAL REPRESENTATIVES

The two major political parties in the United States are the Republican party and the Democratic party. (Q.45).

The political party of the President now is the _____ party. (Q.46)

The name of the Speaker of the House of Representatives is _____. (Q.47)

(Q.20) Who is one of your state's U.S. Senators now?

Answers will vary. (District of Columbia residents and residents of U.S. territories should answer that D.C. (or territory where applicant lives) has no U.S, Senators.

(Q.23) Name your U.S. Representative.

(Residents of territories with nonvoting Delegates or Resident Commissioners may provide the name of the Delegate or Commissioner. Also acceptable is any statement that the territory has no (voting) Representatives in Congress.)

(Q.43) Who is the Governor of your state now?_____ (District of Columbia residents should answer that D.C. does not have a Governor.)

(Q.44) What is the capital of your state?_____(District of Columbia residents should answer that D.C. is not a state and does not have a capital. Residents of U.S. territories should name the Capital of the territory.)

OTHER FAMOUS AMERICANS

Martin Luther King

Martin Luther King fought for civil rights, worked for equality of all Americans. (Q.85) The civil rights movement tried to end discrimination. (Q.84)

Susan B. Anthony fought for women's rights, fought for civil rights. (Q.77)

Benjamin Franklin is famous for being a U.S. diplomat, the oldest member of the Constitutional Convention, first Postmaster General of the United States, writer of "Poor Richard's Almanac, and for starting the first free libraries. (Q.68)

RIGHTS AND RESPONSIBILITIES OF U.S. CITIZENS

A responsibility of an American citizen is 1) to vote in a federal election, and 2) serve on a jury. (Q.49)

Vote Poster

A right of an American Citizen is 1) to vote in a federal election, and 2) run for federal office. (Q.50)

A citizen has to be eighteen (18) or older to vote for President. (Q.54)

Rights of everyone living in the United States are: freedom of expression, freedom of speech, freedom of assembly, freedom to petition the government, freedom of worship, and the right to bear arms. (Q.51)

Promises you make when you become a United States citizen are

1) give up loyalty to other countries

2) defend the Constitution and laws of the United States

3) obey the laws of the United States

4) serve in the U.S. military (if needed)

5) serve (do important work for) the nation (if needed), and

6) be loyal to the United States. (Q.53)

We show loyalty to the flag when we say the Pledge of Allegiance. (Q.52)

Ways that Americans can participate in their democracy are:

1) vote

2) join a political party

3) help with a campaign

4) join a civic group

5) join a community group

6) give an elected official your opinion on an issue

7) call Senators and Representatives

8) publicly support or oppose an issue or policy

9) run for office, and

10) write to a newspaper (Q.55)

The last day to send in a federal tax return is April 15. (Q.56)

All men must register for the selective service at age eighteen (18). (Q.48)

OUR ECONOMIC SYSTEM

In the United States, we believe in freedom to conduct business.

The economic system in the United States is: a capitalist economy, also called a market economy. (Q.11)

CITIZENSHIP TEST PREP

Picture Credits

Indian Village: American Indians, Wikipedia, Public domain, Copyright expired.

Newport Church. Wikipedia. Released into public domain by author Kallicrates.

Constitutional Convention, Wikipedia, Public domain.

Boston Tea Party Stamp. Wikipedia. Public domain.

President and his cabinet. Wikipedia. Public domain work of US government.

United States. States that border Canada and Mexico. Wikipedia. Public domain.

American Flag. Fotolia.com license.

Independence Day Parade. Daniel Ramirez. Wikipedia.com Creative Commons Attribution 2.0 Generic .

Martin Luther King. Wikipedia. Public domain.

VOTE poster. Wikipedia.org. Public domain, published before 1/1/1925.

Pledge of Allegiance. Wikipedia. Public domain work of US.

House of Representative Members
(Congressional Representatives: 435)

Several races were not final as of 11-17-24. The name of the "incumbent" is provided.
The number before each name is the Congressional District number.
Check current names at
https://en.wikipedia.org/wiki/2024_United_States_House_of_Representatives_elections

Projected as of Jan. 2025:

ALABAMA
1 Barry Moore
2 Shomari Figures
3 Mike Rogers
4 Robert B. Aderholt
5 Dale Strong
6 Gary J. Palmer
7 Terri A. Sewell

ALASKA
Mary Pertola (incumbent)

ARIZONA
1 David Schweikert
2 Eli Crane
3 Yassamin Ansari
4 Greg Stanton
5 Andy Biggs
6 Andy Biggs
7 Raul Grijalva
8 Abraham Hamadeh
9 Paul Gosar

ARKANSAS
1 Eric A. "Rick" Crawford
2 J. French Hill
3 Steve Womack
4 Bruce Westerman

CALIFORNIA
1 Doug LaMalfa
2 Jared Huffman
3 Kevin Kiley
4 Mike Thompson
5 Tom McClintock
6 Ami Bera

7. Doris Matsui
8 John Garamendi
9. Josh Harder
10 Mark De Saulnier
11 Nancy Pelosi
12. Lateefah Simon
13. John Duarte (incumbent)
14 Eric Swalwell
15 Kevin Mullen
16 Sam Liccardo
17 Ro Khanna
18 Anna G. Eshoo
19 Jimmy Panetta
20 Vince Fong
21 Jim Costa
22 David Valadao
23 Jay Obernolte
24 Salud O. Carbajal
25 Raul Ruiz
26 Julia Brownley
27 George Whitesides
28 Judy Chu
29 Luz Rivas
30 Laura Friedman
31 Gil Cisneros
32 Brad Sherman
33 Pete Aguilar
34 Jimmy Gomez
35 Norma J. Torres
36 Ted Lieu
37 Sydney Kamlager-Dove
38 Linda T. Sánchez
39 Mark Takano
40 Young Kim
41 Ken Calvert
42 Robert Garcia
43 Maxine Waters
44 Nanette Diaz Barragán
45 Michelle Steel (incumbent)

46 J. Luis Correa
47 Dave Min
48 Darrell Issa
49 Mike Levin
50 Darrell Issa
51 Sara Jacobs
52 Juan Vargas

COLORADO
1 Diana DeGette
2 Joe Neguse
3 Jeff Hurd
4 Lauren Boebert
5 Jeff Crank
6 Jason Crow
7 Brittany Pettersen
8. Gabe Evans

CONNECTICUT
1 John B. Larson
2 Joe Courtney
3 Rosa L. DeLauro
4 James A. Himes
5 Jahana Hayes

DELAWARE
AT LARGE
Sarah McBride

FLORIDA
1 Matt Gaetz
2 Neal P. Dunn
3 Kat Cammack
4 Aaron Bean
5 John Rutherford
6 Michael Waltz
7 Cory Mills
8 Mike Haridopolos
9 Darren Soto

10 Maxwell Frost
11 Daniel Webster
12 Gus M. Bilirakis
13 Anna Paulina Luna
14 Kathy Castor
15 Laurel Lee
16 Vern Buchanan
17 W. Gregory Steube
18 Scott Franklin
19 Byron Donald
20 Sheila Cherfilus-McCormick
21 Brian Mast
22 Lois Frankel
23 Jared Moskowitz
24 Frederica S. Wilson
25 Debbie Wasserman Schultz
26 Mario Diaz-Balart
27 Maria Elvira Salazar
28 Carlos A. Gimenez

GEORGIA
1 Earl L. "Buddy" Carter
2 Sanford D. Bishop, Jr.
3 Brian Jack
4 "Hank" Johnson, Jr.
5 Nikema Williams
6 Lucy McBath
7 Carolyn Bourdeaux
8 Austin Scott
9 Andrew Clyde
10 Mike Collins
11 Barry Loudermilk
12 Rick W. Allen
13 David Scott
14 Marjorie Taylor Greene

HAWAII
1 Ed Case
2 Jill Tokuda

IDAHO
1 Russ Fulcher
2 Michael K. Simpson

ILLINOIS
1 Jonathan Jackson
2 Robin L. Kelly
3 Delia Ramirez
4 Jesús G. "Chuy" García
5 Mike Quigley

6 Sean Casten
7 Danny K. Davis
8 Raja Krishnamoorthi
9 Janice D. Schakowsky
10 Bradley Scott Schneider
11 Bill Foster
12 Mike Bost
13 Nikki Budzinski
14 Lauren Underwood
15 Mary Miller
16 Darin LaHood
17 Eric Sorensen

INDIANA
1 Frank Mrvan
2 Rudy Yakym
3 Maria Stutzman
4 James R. Baird
5 Victoria Spartz
6 Jefferson Shreve
7 André Carson
8 Mark Messner
9 Eric Houchin

IOWA
1 Mariannette Miller-Meeks
2 Ashley Hinson
3 Zach Nunn
4 Randy Feenstra

KANSAS
1 Tracey Mann
2 Derek Schmidt
3 Sharice Davids
4 Ron Estes

KENTUCKY
1 James Comer
2 Brett Guthrie
3 Morgan McGarvey
4 Thomas Massie
5 Harold Rogers
6 Andy Barr

LOUISIANA
1 Steve Scalise
2 Troy Carter
3 Clay Higgins
4 Mike Johnson
5 Julia Letlow

6 Cleo Fields

MAINE
1 Chellie Pingree
2 Jared F. Golden

MARYLAND
1 Andy Harris
2 Johnny Olszewski
3 Sarah Elfreth
4 Glenn Ivey
5 Steny H. Hoyer
6 April McClain-Delaney
7 Kweisi Mfume
8 Jamie Raskin

MASSACHUSETTS
1 Richard E. Neal
2 James P. McGovern
3 Lori Trahan
4 Jake Auchincloss
5 Katherine M. Clark
6 Seth Moulton
7 Ayanna Pressley
8 Stephen F. Lynch
9 William R. Keating

MICHIGAN
1 Jack Bergman
2 John Moolenaar
3 Hillary Scholten
4 Bill Huizenga
5 Tim Walberg
6 Debbie Dingell
7 Tom Barrett
8 Kristen McDonald Rivet
9 Lisa McClain
10 John James
11 Haley M. Stevens
12 Rashida Tlaib
13 Shri Thanedar

MINNESOTA
1 Brad Finstad
2 Angie Craig
3 Kelly Morrison
4 Betty McCollum
5 Ilhan Omar
6 Tom Emmer
7 Michelle Fischbach

8 Pete Stauber

MISSISSIPPI
1 Trent Kelly
2 Bennie G. Thompson
3 Michael Guest
4 Mike Ezell

MISSOURI
1 Cori Bush
2 Ann Wagner
3 Blaine Luetkemeyer
4 Mark Alford
5 Emanuel Cleaver
6 Sam Graves
7 Eric Burlizon
8 Jason Smith

MONTANA
1 Ryan Zinke
2 Troy Downing

NEBRASKA
1 Mike Flood
2 Don Bacon
3 Adrian Smith

NEVADA
1 Dina Titus
2 Mark E. Amodei
3 Susie Lee
4 Steven Horsford

NEW HAMPSHIRE
1 Chris Pappas
2 Maggie Goodlander

NEW JERSEY
1 Donald Norcross
2 Jefferson Van Drew
3 Herb Conaway
4 Christopher H. Smith
5 Josh Gottheimer
6 Frank Pallone, Jr.
7 Tom Keane, Jr.
8 Rob Menedez
9 Nellie Pou
10 LaMonica McIver
11 Mikie Sherrill
12 Bonnie Watson Coleman

NEW MEXICO
1 Melanie Stansbury
2 Gabe Vasquez
3 Teresa Leger Fernandez

NEW YORK
1 Nick LaLota
2 Andre R. Garbarino
3 Thomas R. Suozzi
4 Laura Gillen
5 Gregory W. Meeks
6 Grace Meng
7 Nydia M. Velázquez
8 Hakeem S. Jeffries
9 Yvette D. Clarke
10 Dan Goldman
11 Nicole Malliotakis
12 Jerry Nadler
13 Adriano Espaillat
14 Alexandria Ocasio-Cortez
15 Ritchie Torres
16 George Latimer
17 Mike Lawler
18 Pat Ryan
19 Josh Riley
20 Paul Tonko
21 Elise M. Stefanik
22 John Mannion
23 Nick Langworthy
24 Claudia Tenney
25 Joseph D. Morelle
26 Tim Kennedy

NORTH CAROLINA
1 Don Davis
2 Deborah Ross
3 Greg Murphy
4 Valerie Foushee
5 Virginia Foxx
6 Addison McDowell
7 David Rouzer
8 Mark Harris
9 Richard Hudson
10 Pat Harrigan
11 Chuck Edwards
12 Alma S. Adams
13 Brad Knoww
14 Tim Moore

NORTH DAKOTA
AT LARGE

Kelly Armstrong

OHIO
1 Greg Landsmant
2 David Taylor
3 Joyce Beatty
4 Jim Jordan
5 Robert E. Latta
6 Michael Ruilli
7 Max Miller
8 Warren Davidson
9 Marcy Kaptur
10 Michael R. Turner
11 Shontel Brown
12 Troy Balderson
13 Emilia Sykes
14 David P. Joyce
15 Mike Carey

OKLAHOMA
1 Kevin Hern
2 Josh Brecheen
3 Frank D. Lucas
4 Tom Cole
5 Stephanie Bice

OREGON
1 Suzanne Bonamici
2 Cliff Bentz
3 Maxine Dexter
4 Van Hoyle
5 Janelle Bynum
6 Andrea Salinas

PENNSYLVANIA
1 Brian K. Fitzpatrick
2 Brendan F. Boyle
3 Dwight Evans
4 Madeleine Dean
5 Mary Gay Scanlon
6 Chrissy Houlahan
7 Ryan McKenzie
8 Rob Bresnahan
9 Daniel Meuser
10 Scott Perry
11 Lloyd Smucker
12 Summer Lee
13 John Joyce
14 Guy Reschenthaler
15 Glenn Thompson

16 Mike Kelly
17 Chris Deluzio

RHODE ISLAND
1 Gabe Amo
2 Seth Magaziner

SOUTH CAROLINA
1 Nancy Mace
2 Joe Wilson
3 Sheri Biggs
4 William R. Timmons IV
5 Ralph Norman
6 James E. Clyburn
7 Russell Fry

SOUTH DAKOTA
AT LARGE
Dusty Johnson

TENNESSEE
1 Diana Harshbarger
2 Tim Burchett
3 Charles J. "Chuck" Fleischmann
4 Scott DesJarlais
5 Andy Ogles
6 John W. Rose
7 Mark E. Green
8 David Kustoff
9 Steve Cohen

TEXAS
1 Nathaniel Moran
2 Dan Crenshaw
3 Keith Self
4 Pat Fallon
5 Lance Gooden
6 Jake Elizey
7 Lizzie Fletcher
8 Morgan Luttrell
9 Al Green
10 Michael T. McCaul
11 August Pfluger
12 Craig Goldman
13 Ronny Jackson
14 Randy K. Weber, Sr.
15 Monica De La Cruz
16 Veronica Escobar
17 Pete Sessions

18 Sylvester Turner
19 Jodey C. Arrington
20 Joaquin Castro
21 Chip Roy
22 Troy Nehls
23 Tony Gonzales
24 Beth Van Duyne
25 Roger Williams
26 Brandon Gill
27 Michael Cloud
28 Henry Cuellar
29 Sylvia R. Garcia
30 Jasmine Crockett
31 John R. Carter
32 Julie Johnson
33 Marc A. Veasey
34 Vicente Gonzalez
35 Greg Casar
36 Brian Babin
37 Llyod Doggett
38 Wesley Hunt

UTAH
1 Blake Moore
2 Celeste Maloy
3 Mike Kennedy
4 Burgess Owens

VERMONT
AT LARGE
Becca Balint

VIRGINIA
1 Robert J. Wittman
2 Ken Kiggans
3 Robert C. "Bobby" Scott
4 A. Donald McEachin
5 John McGuire
6 Ben Cline
7 Eugene Vindman
8 Donald S. Beyer, Jr.
9 H. Morgan Griffith
10 Suhas Subramanyam
11 Gerald E. Connolly

WASHINGTON
1 Suzan K. DelBene
2 Rick Larsen
3 Marie Gluesenkamp Perez
4 Dan Newhouse

5 Michael Baumgartner
6 Emily Randall
7 Pramila Jayapal
8 Kim Schrier
9 Adam Smith
10 Marilyn Strickland

WEST VIRGINIA
1 Carol Miller
2 Riley Moore

WISCONSIN
1 Bryan Steil
2 Mark Pocan
3 Derrick Van Orden
4 Gwen Moore
5 Scott Fitzgerald
6 Glenn Grothman
7 Tom Tiffany
8 Tony Wied

WYOMING
AT LARGE
Harriet Hageman

PUERTO RICO
RESIDENT COMMISSIONER
Pablo Hernandez Rivera

AMERICAN SAMOA
DELEGATE
Amata Coleman Radewagen

DISTRICT OF COLUMBIA
DELEGATE
Eleanor Holmes Norton

GUAM
DELEGATE
James Moylan

NORTHERN MARIANA ISLANDS
DELEGATE
Kimberly King-Hinds

VIRGIN ISLANDS
DELEGATEStacey E. Plaskett

US Senators (50 States)

State	Senators	State	Senators
Alabama	1. Tommy Tuberville 2. Katie Britt	**Indiana**	1. Jim Banks 2. Todd Young
Alaska	1. Lisa Murkowski 2. Dan Sullivan	**Iowa**	1. Joni Ernst 2. Chuck Grassley
Arizona	1. Mark Kelly 2. Rube Gallego	**Kansas**	1. Jerry Moran 2. Roger Marshall
Arkansas	1. John Boozman 2. Tom Cotton	**Kentucky**	1. Mitch McConnell 2. Rand Paul
California	1. Adam Schiff 2. Alex Padilla	**Louisiana**	1. Bill Cassidy 2. John Kennedy
Colorado	1. Michael F. Bennett 2. John Hickenlooper	**Maine**	1. Susan M. Collins 2. Angus S. King, Jr.
Connecticut	1. Richard Blumenthal 2. Christopher Murphy	**Maryland**	1. Benjamin Cardin 2. Angela Alsobrooks
Delaware	1. Lisa Blunt Rochester 2. Christopher A. Coons	**Massachusetts**	1. Edward J. Markey 2. Elizabeth D. Warren
Florida	1. To be appointed 2. Rick Scott	**Michigan**	1. Gary C. Peters 2. Elissa Slotkin
Georgia	1. John Ossoff 2. Raphael G. Warnock	**Minnesota**	1. Amy Klobuchar 2. Tina Smith
Hawaii	1. Mazie K. Hirono 2. Brian Schatz	**Mississippi**	1. Cindy Hyde-Smith 2. Roger F. Wicker
Idaho	1. Mike Crapo 2. James E. Risch	**Missouri**	1. Eric Schmitt 2. Josh R. Hawley
Illinois	1. Tammy Duckworth 2. Richard J. Durbin	**Montana**	1. Steve Daines 2. Tim Sheehy

CITIZENSHIP TEST PREP

State	Senators	State	Senators
Nebraska	1. Deb Fischer 2. Pete Ricketts	**South Carolina**	1. Lindsey Graham 2. Tim Scott
Nevada	1. Catherine Cortez Masto 2. Jacky Rosen	**South Dakota**	1. Mike Rounds 2. John Thune
New Hampshire	1. Margaret Wood Hassan 2. Jeanne Shaheen	**Tennessee**	1. Bill Hagerty 2. Marsha Blackburn
New Jersey	1. Cory Booker 2. Robert Menendez	**Texas**	1. John Cornyn 2. Ted Cruz
New Mexico	1. Martin Heinrich 2. Ben Ray Lujan	**Utah**	1. Mike Lee 2. John Curtis
New York	1. Kirsten E. Gillibrand 2. Charles E. Schumer	**Vermont**	1. Peter Welch 2. Bernard Sanders
North Carolina	1. Thom Tillis 2. Ted Budd	**Virginia**	1. Tim Kaine 2. Mark R. Warner
North Dakota	1. Kevin Cramer 2. John Hoeven	**Washington**	1. Maria Cantwell 2. Patty Murray
Ohio	1. Bernie Moreno 2. To be appointed	**West Virginia**	1. Shelley Moore Capito 2. Jim Justice
Oklahoma	1. Markwayne Mullin 2. James Lankford	**Wisconsin**	1. Tammy Baldwin 2. Ron Johnson
Oregon	1. Jeff Merkley 2. Ron Wyden	**Wyoming**	1. John Barrasso 2. Cynthia Lummis
Pennsylvania	1. Robert P. Casey, Jr. 2. John Fetterman		
Rhode Island	1. Jack Reed 2. Sheldon Whitehouse		

State Capitals (50) and Territories

State	Capital City
Alabama	Montgomery
Alaska	Juneau
Arizona	Phoenix
Arkansas	Little Rock
California	Sacramento
Colorado	Denver
Connecticut	Hartford
Delaware	Dover
Florida	Tallahassee
Georgia	Atlanta
Hawaii	Honolulu
Idaho	Boise
Illinois	Springfield
Indiana	Indianapolis
Iowa	Des Moines
Kansas	Topeka
Kentucky	Frankfort
Louisiana	Baton Rouge
Maine	Augusta
Maryland	Annapolis
Massachusetts	Boston
Michigan	Lansing
Minnesota	St. Paul
Mississippi	Jackson
Missouri	Jefferson City
Montana	Helena
Nebraska	Lincoln
Nevada	Carson City

State	Capital City
New Hampshire	Concord
New Jersey	Trenton
New Mexico	Santa Fe
New York	Albany
North Carolina	Raleigh
North Dakota	Bismarck
Ohio	Columbus
Oklahoma	Oklahoma City
Oregon	Salem
Pennsylvania	Harrisburg
Rhode Island	Providence
South Carolina	Columbia
South Dakota	Pierre
Tennessee	Nashville
Texas	Austin
Utah	Salt Lake City
Vermont	Montpelier
Virginia	Richmond
Washington	Olympia
West Virginia	Charleston
Wisconsin	Madison
Wyoming	Cheyenne
U.S. Territories (#) Partial List	
American Samoa	Pago Pago
Guam	Hagatna
Northern Mariana Islands	Saipan
Puerto Rico	San Juan
U.S. Virgin Islands	Charlotte Amalie

State Governors (50) and Territories

State	Governor	State	Governor
Alabama	Kay Ivey	New Hampshire	Chris Sununu
Alaska	Michael J. Dunleavy	New Jersey	Phil Murphy
Arizona	Katie Hobbs	New Mexico	Michelle Lujan Grisham
Arkansas	Sarah Huckabee Sanders	New York	Cathy Hochul
California	Gavin Newsom	North Carolina	Roy Cooper
Colorado	Jared Polis	North Dakota	Doug Burgum
Connecticut	Ned Lamont	Ohio	Mike DeWine
Delaware	John Carney	Oklahoma	Kevin Stitt
Florida	Ron DeSantis	Oregon	Tina Kotek
Georgia	Brian P. Kemp	Pennsylvania	Josh Shapiro
Hawaii	Josh Green	Rhode Island	Dan McKee
Idaho	Brad Little	South Carolina	Henry McMaster
Illinois	JB Pritzker	South Dakota	Kristi Noem
Indiana	Eric J. Holcomb	Tennessee	Bill Lee
Iowa	Kim Reynolds	Texas	Greg Abbott
Kansas	Laura Kelly	Utah	Spencer Cox
Kentucky	Andy Beshear	Vermont	Phil Scott
Louisiana	Jeff Landry	Virginia	Glenn Youngkin
Maine	Janet Mills	Washington	Jay Inslee
Maryland	Wes Moore	West Virginia	Jim Justice
Massachusetts	Maura Healey	Wisconsin	Tony Evers
Michigan	Gretchen Whitmer	Wyoming	Mark Gordon
Minnesota	Tim Walz	U.S. Territories (#) Partial List	
Mississippi	Jonathan Tate Reeves	American Samoa	Lemanu P.S. Mauga
Missouri	Mike Parson	Guam	Lourdes (Lou) A. Leon Guerrero
Montana	Greg Gianforte	Northern Mariana Islands	Arnold Palacios
Nebraska	Pete Ricketts	Puerto Rico	Pedro Pierluisi
Nevada	Steve Sisolak	U.S. Virgin Islands	Albert Bryan

Getting Information Online

1. U.S. Immigration and Naturalization Services' web page (for learning about becoming a U.S. citizen) is at:

www.uscis.gov/citizenship

----

2. FREE citizenship (naturalization) interview example video

FREE USCIS video (which has an example of the interview):

www.uscis.gov/citizenship/learn-about-citizenship/the-naturalization-interview-and-test

----

3.To get Citizenship test question and answer updates, go to:

www.uscis.gov/citizenship/testupdates

----

4. Names of the 2 United States Senators from your State:

www.senate.gov/senators

See "Find Your Senators" at the top left of the screen.

----

5. Name of your state's Governor:

www.usa.gov/states-and-territories

----

6. Name of your Representative and the name of the Speaker of the House of Representatives: (Click "Representatives")

www.house.gov

Made in the USA
Coppell, TX
10 December 2024

42131334R00059